SCHIRMER'S LIBRARY
OF MUSICAL CLASSICS

CHARLES DANCLA

Airs Variés

For the Violin

With Piano Accompaniment

Edited by

LOUIS SVEĆENSKI

IN TWO SERIES

→ FIRST SERIES

Library Vol. 785 — Op. 89

G. SCHIRMER, Inc.

DISTRIBUTED BY

HAL•LEONARD
CORPORATION

7777 W. BLUEMOUND RD. P.O. BOX 13819 MILWAUKEE, WI 53213

1er Air Varié
on a theme by Pacini

Edited by Louis Svećenski

Charles Dancla. Op. 89, No. 1

Theme
Moderato

Variation
Moderato

dolce e con eleganza

f marcato

Coda

2ᵐᵉ Air Varié
on a theme by Rossini

Edited by Louis Svećenski

Charles Dancla. Op. 89. No. 2

Var. II
Brillante

Coda

3me Air Varié
on a theme by Bellini

Edited by Louis Svećenski

Charles Dancla. Op. 89, No. 3

Theme
Moderato cantabile

Var. I

Var. II
Risoluto

Coda

4me Air Varié
on a theme by Donizetti

Edited by Louis Svećenski

Charles Dancla. Op. 89, No. 4

Violin

SCHIRMER'S LIBRARY
OF MUSICAL CLASSICS

CHARLES DANCLA

Airs Variés

For the Violin

With Piano Accompaniment

Edited by

LOUIS SVEĆENSKI

IN TWO SERIES

→ FIRST SERIES

Library Vol. 785 — Op. 89

SECOND SERIES

Library Vol. 1431 — Op. 118

G. SCHIRMER, Inc.

DISTRIBUTED BY

7777 W. BLUEMOUND RD. P.O. BOX 13819 MILWAUKEE, WI 53213

1er Air Varié
on a theme by Pacini

Violin

Edited by Louis Svećenski

Charles Dancla. Op. 89, No. 1

Andante maestoso

Theme
Moderato *fieramente (boldly)*

Violin

2me Air Varié
on a theme by Rossini

Violin

Edited by Louis Svećenski

Charles Dancla. Op. 89, No. 2

3me Air Varié
on a theme by Bellini

Violin

Edited by Louis Svećenski

Charles Dancla. Op. 89, No. 3

Violin

4me Air Varié
on a theme by Donizetti

Violin

Edited by Louis Svećenski

Charles Dancla. Op. 89, No. 4

Violin

9

5me Air Varié
on a theme by Weigl

Edited by Louis Svećenski

Violin

Charles Dancla. Op. 89, No. 5

Cantabile

pizz.

harm.

cantabile

pizz.

cresc.

pizz.

pizz.

Tempo animato

Più facile

6me Air Varié
on a theme by Mercadante

Violin

Edited by Louis Svećenski

Charles Dancla. Op. 89, No. 6

Theme

Andante maestoso Andante cantabile

Var. I
Un poco più animato

Var. II
Cantabile *con eleganza*

Var. III
Brillante

Var. II
Allegro moderato

poco rit.   a tempo

5me Air Varié
on a theme by Weigl

Edited by Louis Svećenski

Charles Dancla. Op. 89, No. 5

Var. II
Brillante

molto stacc.

pizz.

Tempo animato

leggiero

Più facile

cresc.

6me Air Varié
on a theme by Mercadante

Edited by Louis Svećenski

Charles Dancla. Op. 89, No. 6

Var. I
Un poco più animato

Var. II
Cantabile

Var. III
Brillante